sky

lion

[a narrative poetry.]

This is a work of fiction.
Names, characters, businesses, places, events, locales, and incidents are either the products of the author's imagination or used in a fictitious manner. Any resemblance to actual persons, living or dead, or actual events is purely coincidental.

Copyright © 2018 Loni McWilliams
All rights reserved.
ISBN: 9781790664771

loni mcwilliams

.

DEDICATION & ACKNOWLEDGEMENTS

for Dorcas Camacho, the original **sky lion.**
i know in my heart that there is a reason for everything.
my reason for this [and every other act of courage] is you.

to ang, my go-to,
who has begged me to do this since silver trail middle,
and her young king on the way.
you don't have to solemnly believe in my message like you do,
or fiercely protect my energy for these 16 years like you do…but you do.
none of this would be any fun or make any sense
without my second self.

to tabby - more than a sister.
you are both the muse and the editor. you are my poetry in motion.

i'd like to pay respects to David "Weston Mac" McWilliams
pops, via bonfire poetry & canvas paintings,
you were the very first creative influence in my life.
i can only pray you dive into this and feel proud of your role in it's birth.

to the angels at San Diego Writer's Ink…
every literary genius who paved the way for me..
the kindred spirits that come alive for language…
to you. *(yes, you.)*
from the writer's block to the oversharing,
i hope that if my content ever resonates,
it speaks the merit that is living your whole truth
by being 100% honest with your passion
& watching that authenticity organically spill over into parts of your life
that go far beyond this physical dimension.
these pages are a concrete manifestation of my personal journey to that goal.
know that if i can do this,
anyone can.

to God be the glory.

yours in ink,

CONTENTS BY SECTION

a message from me to you

//the pieces of poetry & prose that you'll find between these covers
have been a work in progress since i was in
michelle watson's fourth grade english language arts class
where i was first challenged to dig deeper
using language as my tool
& on some days
my ammunition
a select few are reworks or excerpts dated as far back as 1999 /

every feeling i've fought
or embraced
between then & now
can be found in the depths of some worn & tattered notebook
this passion project is my best attempt at collecting the ones i believe have molded
shaped
influenced
my personal growth the most
& stringing them into a sequence i can consider worthy of sharing /
i'm aware most people don't believe in getting this intimate with the world -
or even with themselves -
i've been that person too
i'm learning that when you have a message on your heart
it's just different..
it's already the most liberating decision of my life /

i've evolved through several different versions of my Self along this path
& in certain instances
channeled what family or friends were going through
to convey things that they were struggling to put into words
you know who you are -
i'm forever grateful that you'd trust me enough
to let me turn your lessons into literature /

with this said
i risk the probable chance
that by the time these reach your eyes
i will have altogether outgrown the spirit who birthed them
or naturally
the writers risk of overall misinterpretation
but omitting portions i've outgrown
would be undermining their place in the journey

so i suppose that's the beauty of it
& hopefully it will serve as incentive
to continue documenting all the stages of the evolution
that may never have otherwise been preserved
recreated
or fully understood /

each lowercase letter of each word
each use of punctuation or lack thereof
each bolded or italicized text
each line break
each misplaced period
each oceanic reference
each title at each finish line
each format
each page turn
each run-on sentence
each chapter
within each cloud
symbolizing a different component of the inevitable life cycle -
from the severe thunderstorm
to the overcast
to the sunshine
to the ultimate roar of the sky lion's ascension...
every last melodramatic message
that enabled this vision to come to fruition
was precisely calculated
to generate a response from both you & i
to feel
to think
to vibe
to simply be still with yourself
to dig just a tiny bit deeper
if nothing else..
ideally
to create a safe space
within the pages
to flow freely with the essence of these notions
without the need to control or judge your own reactions
whether they be positive
negative
or neutral /

this was & still is
the inside process that made this project come to life
& also afforded me the courage to share it with you
with the hope that i could transfer even a fraction
of that sense of liberation to my readers -
that is -
the liberation of being *human*
as messy & raw as that can get /
whether or not we achieve this...well
that's a perpetual work in progress
but in the meantime
i appreciate you for giving my craft a chance /
all of the little girls & grown women who have lived in my body
& used it as a vessel for self-expression
are thanking me for doing this
& thanking you for letting me /

some of my greatest inspirations have been the artists
who get so honest about their troubles that it makes us uncomfortable /
i believe there's something to be said about those brave enough
to publicize their storms
in a way that reminds us we're never alone in the rain /

the reality i'm now embracing is that much of what i've composed over the years
was originally inspired by some sort of pain
& it's metamorphosis into higher vibrations /
what may be difficult for you to read
was difficult for me to write
but what you're holding is my very own therapy /

i made a vow to myself that my work would honor the celebrations & tribulations alike...
that i tell the stories on my heart -
not to impress -
but rather
because this divine journey continues to impress *me*..

so whether you come here for soul soothing
recreational reading
or just friendly support
i hope you find yourself reminded
that the greatest empowerment of our existence
is how we can turn our misery into magic /

lastly
to align with the attitude that i try to maintain towards everything on this journey
i ask that you don't take it too seriously /

after all
this life is so much more whimsical
than our heavy human experience gives it credit for //

-project intention//
prelude

inhale the script
in a voice that soothes you;
know that all is well.

-embarking

PART I:
THE CLOUDS

[if the storys too much for the sane,
  let the psychos tell it-
  let us flirt with the pain
  off the psychadelics…]

CUMU*LON*IMBUS

chapter 1

Large, puffy, dark clouds associated with heavy
rainfall // Indicative of severe thunderstorms,
lightning, damaging winds & tornadoes.

pay attention to the irony
that is the appetite of your soul
(it makes it's own rules, after all.)

a mere taste of what is for you
will leave you satisfied /
heaping portions of what is not
will leave you famished.

-for the healing & heart starved

my religiously indoctrinated father
my free spirited eagle of a mother
they never agreed
yet they were both always right
-the fight

you have these eyes
the deepest of blues
glittering like seawater
under summer sun

the softer sex
they are all impressed.
lusting for a glance.
or a chance.
at romance.

perhaps that's how you forgot -
i've got the whole ocean in my veins

-reasons i left (2018)

(spoken word, slam poetry & freestyle standup;
San Diego, CA. 2018.)
modeling agent says "you're drop dead gorgeous BUT you're too 'thick.'
lose twenty pounds and the aesthetic will fit."
like he can love me for my green eyes but not my childbearing hips
like if i looked malnourished, then i'd be legit.
i put it like this..

i come from poets with rhymes dripping off sea-salted lips
from prickly sea urchins and freudian slips
the poorest of ghettos, the richest of rich..

from european royalty and latin sensations
women made of stars with curves that map constellations
immigrants reaching shore, roaring celebration
from a fathers frustration
his family lacking foundation
as refugees - brand new to this foreign nation
political infrastructure forced them into migration
failing them beyond your privileged imagination

orchids blooming vibrantly in the midst of spring
hummingbirds, hushed, but continuing to sing
from the innovators, trailblazers, pioneers of ink
the gentlemen and scholars who've now gone extinct
the feminists who flew after they snatched their wings
sailors in 60-foot storm waves... but that boat ain't sink.

from prayers in the cockpit, fights with the mast
salt on their breath, eyes made of sea glass
from voluptuous forms of beauty that you fail to consider
women with physiques the Lord molded to deliver
societies that never shamed them for not being thinner
the ones who took major losses but still only breed winners
peace advocates with the pen as their trigger…

from sun-weathered ocean skin
so-called saints still seasoned in sin
from prophets and priests and their journeys within
those who laid down their weapons but *never their pens*

from a rich history of queens
who kept the throne clean
who fought for their daughters to be heard, not just seen
from metaphysical to concrete to all that's between

sir, who the fuck are you to figure
that the scale should be a measure or a predictor
to size up a woman and say how you could fix her
and tweak her to meet societies picture

i come from a lineage of defeats followed by triumphant glories
my hips are wide **because they're full of stories**

-history of queens
[spoken word & freestyle standup;
san diego, CA. 2018.]

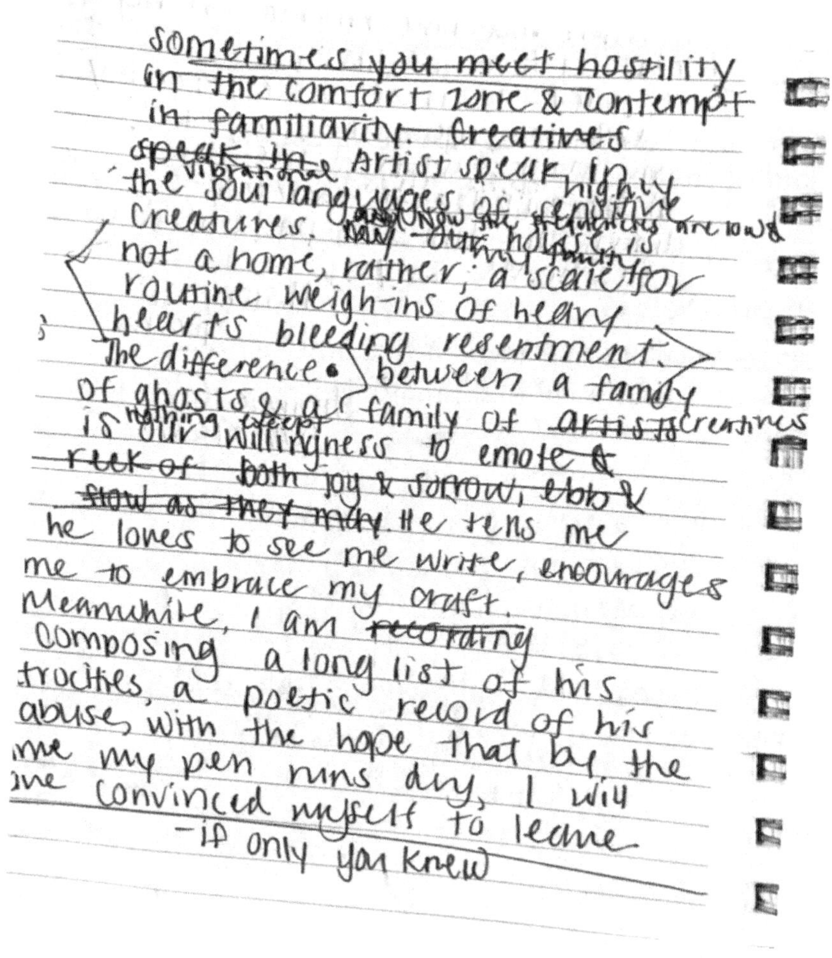

[handwritten note:]

sometimes you meet hostility
in the comfort zone & contempt
in familiarity. creatives
speak the artist speak highly
the vibrational
the soul languages of creatives
creatures. Now the residents are loud
is not a home, rather; a scale for
routine weigh-ins of heavy
hearts bleeding resentment.
The difference. between a family
of ghosts & a family of artists creatives
is nothing except our willingness to emote &
reek of both joy & sorrow, ebb &
flow as they may. He tells me
he loves to see me write, encourages
me to embrace my craft.
Meanwhile, I am recording
composing a long list of his atrocities, a poetic record of his
abuse, with the hope that by the
time my pen runs dry, I will
have convinced myself to leave.
—if only you knew

he tells me he loves to see me write
encourages me to embrace my art

meanwhile.
i am composing a long list of his atrocities
a poetic record of his abuse
with the intention that by the time my ink runs dry
i will have convinced myself to leave
-if you only knew (2016)

my first love
pulls food out of the ocean /
pulls poetic rhymes out of thin air /
serenades me with island tunes /
has the holy scriptures committed to memory /
his prayers are unmatched.

taller than the tales i told him as a teen /
broad as these dreams that i don't reckon he cares to believe in.
-sweet pops

first it was water in the midst of a drought

then it was death by tsunami

quenching my thirst

bringing vitality back to all of my cities

right before drowning me in waves

-toxic romance

You daydream out loud
about owning all of my
tomorrows
How should I confess..
I scarcely want your today.
  -love breach

-love breach

today i cried with my nail lady..

i sit down
and she chirps
in her thickest vietnamese accent
"lo, you look tide.
you look worry…

silence

you ok?"

turns out a fresh tan and some mascara
can't hide my empty.

and she wept with me.
told me how she worries
for mother's life daily /
has night terrors
knowing she's unsafe
crossing the street in their motherland /
holds her breath
breaks a tiny sweat
each time vietnam shows up
on the caller ID /

and she let it bleed out with me
as she massaged my hand
with all the tenderness of a woman
whose hands are no stranger to pain /

"one day at a time, bay-bee.
one day at a time." /

and in the company of a perfect stranger
was the first time all day
i felt maybe i was safe
to feel this fear
to own this ugly
to drop the mask
even for just a fleeting moment /

today i cried with my nail lady
because the best thing i am
is your daughter -
what will be my best thing if you leave?

-today we found out you have parkinson's
[09.18.2018]

a moment with my anatomy
or perhaps a few
this blessed body is a cloud
releasing her water
heavy with dew

she can't find it in her
wet with rain
to identify
with implicit disapproval
misplaced shame

this cloud does not have
the energy

the intention

the commitment
for tears

instead i think she will climax
and label it "self-love"
-my bedside drawer

it's 3:44am

i woke up to write of you

you'll wake up reeking of her

-the difference

was FLOATING
& pure
now GROPING
for more
CHOKING
& sore
PROVOKING
ignored
IMPLODING
for sure
EMOTING
~~what~~ what's more
WROTE THINGS
~~therefore~~ therefore
HOPE CLINGS
what for
— the process

-the process

rub salt in their wound

the very wound you sliced.

ignore the scar tissue;

label it another lesson.

tell them t h i s i s *l* o v e.

if for long enough

and with enough conviction

perhaps you will both begin to believe it

-instructions for manipulation

my word is bond
so i don't promise much
but i promise this

i will forgive you in time /
i will let freedom make sweet love to your past /
i will invigorate your deepest regrets -
your most threatening secrets -
with the empowerment of being human /

i will give you
permission
to be inherently flawed /

just not today.
-letter to my Self

you will meet eyes
and plenty hearts
that lack scar tissue

they will seem gorgeously shallow
and mostly
effortless to stare into /

yet
you will find them hard to read
and harder, yet, to connect with /

you are much too colossal
to fall into shallow depths /
much too substantial
to lose yourself in hollow spaces /
you have little in common
with the absence of scars /

where there was rain
there are flowers
and honey -
flowing /
where there was pain
there is power
and love -
abundant /

none have ever lived there.
-perfectly incompatible

my heart still weighs heavy with guilt
when i imagine this life treated you so maliciously
that you no longer felt at peace living it

that in your most desperate moments
you searched frantically
in vain
never quite encountering
a sheltered sanctuary
within all the spaces of your spirit -
the mazes of your mind

may your existence in all of the lives to come
feel something like a
safe
free
organic journey back home
[something so much more than just worthy of living]
-suicide angel
(2011)

["...we're blasting carter III in the front of your SUV
-but you'll still call it a truck
mrs. officer, mrs. officer, save my friend for me,
he's about to self-destruct.."]

// excerpt from *long distance (2012)* //

…the nerve
of land and sea
to rest themselves
so inconveniently
between our affection
-worlds away

I come from the
gentlemen & scholars

* look up: Barbara Ras.

.pay   · Bde Every sorrow
attention   · weight of water
to what   · forever buoyant
they tell   · who knows what
you to forget   · all bright & beautiful
-sailors, poets,   humans seek fire & fuel
queens,   but all you want is ash.
pioneers,   · pull that trigger!!
immigrants,   · some lost heaven,
the ghettos &   newfound hell
  the riches,   · ironic how your mouth gets
the stars,   angry every @ me
constellations   every time it says a
child-bearing   lie; ironic how
hips, scotch
freudian   I gotta pretend to
  slips.   believe you cause if
orchids,   not you start to cry.
hummingbrds.   (the pen is my
                              trigger
                              →somehow I'd rather
                              play myself then
                              see   tears
lil. jah.   welling fables in
  bitch.   your eyes

"..ironic how your mouth gets angry @ **me** every time it tells a lie..
then i pretend to believe it cause if not you'll start to cry…
somehow i'd rather play us both than see tears well in your eyes."
-fables

how.
did we.
get here.

cause these days
i'm saying far too much
but never saying nothing new
and you say so fuckin little
but that says a lot too.

how.
did i.
get here.

cause these days
"i love you" feels like
a foreign object in my mouth
but your pulsing body doesn't
so i take it down south

-estranged

in shark infested waters
you are piggy backing on me

your leg gushing blood

i would rather tend to your wounds

then save my own life

is this what they meant

by **"loyal to a fault?"**

-my love is a liability

i raised my weapons high
against countless so-called adversaries -
went to bat for a fallacy
that i would naively mistake for love

the most futile
empty
ludicrous battle
being the war against myself
-white flag

quarter past midnight
i'm gazing at your heart
you're too high to know it

all of it's cunning faces
the salt it pumps
where blood once flowed
the legs it's grown
where the chambers once functioned
the run.
run.
run from reality.
the softness it denies.
the treachery it labels as affection.
the take.
take.
take.

even peering at it
under the magnifying glass
of our so-called love
all i can see
is the hate that once
swallowed it whole
-damaged goods (2017)

here's to each time

good love knocked emphatically

on my bad door

so i gently drew the blinds

and pretended no one was home

-*avoidance//*

timing (2018)

12am looks like writers block

1am penning pain

2:15 dozing off

ink leaking on the sheets

3am silent slumber

4am looks like cold sweats

gritted teeth

breathy whispers of desperation

a silence that isn't quiet

4:15 looks like a hungry young boy

hugging bony knees

head tilted to the heavens

harassing God for answers

-insomniac

the plateaus are one good beer
a half hug
neutral and content
but i could still use a bit more

the lows
the lows are exhausting
a slap across the face
a slam against the wall

i'm tired

so tired

your soul

it's selfish
it's cruel
my skin
it burns

it crawls

you are hideous

stopityouarehurtingme

i hate you

i am trapped
i cannot recognize the one i love
waiting desperately on the day
my affection makes it's quiet exit

[as if that's how it works
as if i'll wake up one day and my love will vanish
as if i've ever enjoyed the finality of putting a lover out of my heart for good]

there goes my mind playing it's go-to trick

but the highs
those highs
are so
so
high.
-addict

i can hear him
screaming

seething

"look at me.

LOOK. AT. ME."

why can't i bring myself to raise my head.
fixate my vision on my makeshift bookmark -
a photo
of my wiser
more intuitive
childhood self

because i know

and he knows

and most of all

she knows…

my eyes won't lock with wandering ones

-treason

i am penning-
for the damsels who were praised for bearing the strength of a lion
yet embarrassed for having it's heart /

i am recording-
for the goddesses who camouflaged their softness
as if it never gave birth to their magic /
who were conditioned to be ashamed of their bosom
as if it never nourished their offspring /

i am emoting-
for the little girls who spent their youths apologizing
for not yet being women
and the women who weren't little girls for long enough /

i am creating-
for the men - the warriors –
raising their daughters on thrones
and the men who were forced to raise themselves /

i am pioneering-
for the unbroken minorities
with greater moral responsibility to positively influence /
for the resilience of their spirits
that will recalibrate histories false notions /

i am exhaling light-
for the trees that supplied shade
for our forefathers to rest under
wisdom for them to sip slowly
roots for them to manifest
wood for them to ignite /

i am documenting-
for those same ancestors
who never had these privileges
yet stood on one another's shoulders
sacrificing wholeheartedly
to leave behind a legacy of opportunities
never once fearing
that they would inevitably watch us squander them
-my why

Talks w/ myself, looks within
@ the life i've been choosing
asking it ~~even~~ "really bout to win
or just look good losing
you fuck w/ yourself?
Then ~~why~~ why the uncertainty ~~#~~
why this ~~habit~~ of self-sabotaging inadvertently?
up in church talking to God
tryna "see things clearer"
just to go home to a fraud
can't look himself in the mirror   flawed
Now your own reflection ~~so~~ looking ~~fucked up~~
Thats cause low-key you fear her
the face looking ~~back~~ @ you recently
you can't recognize her frequency
pray ~~#~~ this season teaches
you patience...   vibrations...
meditating on a day w/ higher
Blast some ms. Lauryn Hill,
~~yet~~ let her verses ~~set~~ your
frustration...
But you haven't learned STILL
THIS YOUR MISEDUCATION
            —The miseducation of
                        Lomac

...talks with myself, look within
at the life i've been choosing
asking if i'm really bout to win
or just look good losing /

you fuck with yourself?
then why the uncertainty..
why this habit of
self-sabotaging inadvertently /

up in church talking to God
tryna "see things clearer"
just to go home to a fraud
can't look himself in the mirror
now your own reflection looking flawed
cause lowkey you fear her ...
the face looking back at you recently
you can't recognize her frequency /

praying this season teaches you patience
meditating on a vision of higher vibrations
blast some ms. lauryn hill
let her verses spit your frustration
but you haven't learned STILL
this your miseducation /
-the miseducation of lo mac
[excerpt from spoken word & freestyle standup recording;
san diego, CA. 2018.]

"i would never do that to you. i love you."
　　-"iloveyoutoo" i blurt

my obsession with pretty
bow-tied words
and how quickly they depreciate in value

and maybe
for that split second afterwards
i have one foot in my mouth
and the other out the door

maybe i'm in love
with an abandoned
lost puppy
dressed up in big boys clothing

maybe his lie
is as deep as his fear
that ultimately
i love me
entirely too much
to let myself believe it.
-going, going, gone

day 44
i'm still struggling to fathom
the wetness of another mouth
on any of my lips
-outdated allegiance

i made a cozy home of his hell
and failed to create an emergency exit.
-let me out of my love

stomping through sloppy stanzas
of lies to myself

casually trailing my mud-drenched boots
through our dialogue

that's how i outgrew your love.

i'm still scrubbing the stains i left.
muttering apologies for the mess.

-when forgiving yourself is harder

may 9, 2009 was your 53rd birthday

when i ran to you for solace

four years ago today

i received the most traumatic phone call of my young adult life

you knew

i was confused and afraid

before i ever gathered the strength to speak /

you knew

my sorrow

before my heart had the chance to process it /

you knew

why i was clutching your immense

callused hands so hard

my knuckles lost all feeling /

you knew

before my knees buckled

 as if those repulsive words –

 "he's gone" –

took the strength with them

as soon as they exited my mouth /

you knew

that was the first time the sanctuary of your arms

could no longer provide me safety /

you knew

more than i did

that i would never in this lifetime be restored

of the innocence that was just stripped of me /

that day
on my 18th year
was the first and only time
i would witness my warrior father
transform into a helpless ball of tears /

not a single tear was shed in front of me
for the loss of his own father
nor when cancer conquered his best friend
nor the expiration date of his 23-year marriage /

none of these events
he was so personally connected too
so emotionally invested in
could drive him to reveal
even the slightest glimpse
of his own human, natural vulnerability
to his youngest daughter /

channeling his baby girl's grief
was the only havoc that could disable him
from the inside out /

in your heart of hearts

you knew

i never had to manage a word

-a fathers empathy (2013)

Today I shed a tear
thinking bout my own father
& how violent he'd get ~~knowing~~ knowing
your dirt on his daughter
how disappointed he'd be that I even
bother
to ~~mmm~~ mess w/ a boy who never
learned honor
How he ~~warned~~ warned me that ~~about~~ boys who
never ~~got used to~~ identified with the grip of their
father -
or the warmth of their whisper,
tend to let that example become
a predictor
another ~~stereotypical~~ stereotypically
weak male figure
the genetically toxic who leave
good women bitter
my father would blame yours
for breeding a quitter

statistically
cursed

today i shed a tear
thinking bout my own father
& how violent he'd get
knowing your dirt on his daughter/
how disappointed he'd be that i even bother
to mess with a boy who never learned honor/
how he warned me that when boys
never identify with the grip of their father-
or the warmth of their whisper-
they tend to let that example become a predictor/
another stereotypically weak male figure/
the genetically toxic who leave good women bitter/
my pops would blame yours for breeding a quitter.
-statistically cursed

all love lost
we both know when /
today your skin
it soaks in sin /
air breathes thick
trust feels thin /
who we are
ain't who we've been /
you caved in
the devil grinned /
web of lies you spin
i devoured it in,
dripping down my chin /
the fighter within
won't give in /
put faith in Him
trust truth to win /

.

.

.

.

.

.

.

.

begin *again.*

-inferno

[spoken word stand-up]

the opposite of self-love
is not self-loathing

but the selfless sacrifice of your Self

to the selfish.

-a special kind of hell

loni, are you breathing?   avocados   Utal
- I'm forgetting how.   arugula/romaine   North
Have you been talking to God?   romaine   South
- I'm afraid he's disappointed   creamer   Washi
loni, are you hurting?   black beans
- I think I must be numb.   cucumbers
- And that boy you love?   wheat pasta
He gave up on loving me   paper towels
- doesn't know how to   quinoa
- do you still love him? Forever post-its   gummy I'm sorry
- loni, you give up on you? never
love is my only frame
of reference for "forever"
in this life - everything else expires. EVERYTHING
                        everything.

TOMMY ≡ HILFIGER

*Love is my only frame of reference for 'forever' in this life-
everything else expires.*

-*"loni, are you breathing?"*
    -*"i'm forgetting how."*
"have you been talking to God?"
    -*"i'm afraid he's disappointed now."*

-*"loni, are you hurting?"*
    -*"i think i must be numb"*
-*"you have to let me hold you*
when the feeling comes."

"loni, and that boy who loved you?"
    "he gave up.. 'cause he knew"
-*"what did he know?"*
    -*"he knew he didn't know how too."*

"tell me the truth,
do you still love him?
    -forever."*

- *"loni............*
*do **you** give up on you?"*
    -*"never."*

-mother/daughter dialogue

i cannot be that hard to love.
you cannot be this easy to hate.
-aftermath

there is a violent storm
inhabiting my body

lightning in my mind
floods in my eyes
thunder in my bones
rumble in my blood

perhaps
when the downpour subsides
and the fog clears
i will take my Self back
giving her permission to embark
on the ascension she so deserves
-rainy heart

STRATUS

chapter 2

When the storm begins to settle, these clouds resemble a layer of gray blanketing the sky. They sit low and may cause heavy fog // Associated with overcast days and light precipitation.

when your fists are clenched
and your voice is hoarse
from screaming a message of peace
that the opposition refuses to hear

be gentle with your journey
stay soft through the battle

He is faithful
you are His vessel
your vindication is pending
-the trial

//excerpt from 'florida's two week notice'//

[kissed the wrong mouth
a combined taste of unspoken guilt
stale perspiration
shitty cologne

i spit him out violently
then hastily came back for seconds]
-bad boy

how many compliments
how many double taps
how many admiring audiences
how many rounds of applause
how many nods of approval
how many unsolicited catcalls
men drooling.
woman flattering.
heads turning.
how many apologies for being you

you
who have crawled this far
loved this hard
lived this intimately
given this selflessly

how many
how many

what is the alternative metric system
that will fill your cup of self-value to its brim
and wake you up out of your self-loathing slumber
so that you are finally whole enough
to celebrate yourself?
-modern day woman

i was born with a bible in my pocket
and a scripture on my tongue
spoon-fed a hearty diet of holy knowledge
discerning right vs. wrong …

this is why i am trapped.
this is why i am free.
-knocking on doors

you see...
i spent my whole life convinced
that my energy alone
could turn grime into gold

i manifested this into my truth
as everything i touched
would burn with more brightness
strike with more strength
bloom with more beauty

i softly identified with this reality
subconsciously made it my peace

imagine the fierce fight i fought
when the universe contradicted my science
as she insisted over and over
that i could not wave my wand
and turn him honorable
-faulty magic

saltwater is the fragrance of your sweat

the waves cradled you from the womb

your favorite poem pages sprinkled in sand

polished by the memory of your searches

for the perfectly dulled shard of sea glass

you locked hands with a lover

who never learned to rock

back and forth

to the rhythm of the Atlantic

yet

you wonder how your heart grew seasick

-cut from a different cloth//

daughter of a sailor

sometimes i tread backwards in time
only to silently apologize to him
for my part in conceiving our bird
knowing i was unprepared for her flight
then impulsively clipping her wings
before ever giving her the chance to soar
-short lived romance

the first time my heart cracked

tabitha told me

1. feelings are waves, loni. they rise and they fall.

2. how you experience them is still up to you.

3. you can avoid them temporarily.

   know that the next one is bound to catch you off guard.

i've celebrated with obnoxious enthusiasm

i've mourned with inconsolable grief

i've let myself ride each wave

the rise

the climax

the plummeting fall of it all

here's what i've found;

1. you will not be a prisoner of anything in this life

   if you refuse to perceive it as a punishment.

   let's not just tolerate the inevitable. let's welcome it.

2. they say humans are 60% water.

   you are more than just a subject of the natural ebb and flow.

   you are the swell in motion, after all.

3. they stand corrected.

   water is the only thing i am.

   -lady wave

when the seed was planted
and the womb was ripe
did we honor her body
her spirit
her create
create
create /

when you clutched the rose
as romance found your voyage
did you salute your original teacher of love
her emote
emote
emote /

when that mirror shattered
glass shards scattered
who praised her fixing
her mend
mend
mend /

when the dove perched on your window sill
peace returned home
did we grant her due credit
her soothe
soothe
soothe /

when our river ran bone dry
the means were exhausted
who wiped her sweat
kissed her hands
her toil
toil
toil /

when the rain came pouring
and the soil seeped
in tears of her grieving offspring
yet
she peeled her body out of bed -
backbone coated in concrete -
did we bow our heads in thanks
her nurture
nurture
nurture /

when the Lord constructs a ladder
grants her the power to ascend
who applauds her
for leading the way
her climb
climb
climb /

and when winters grew frigid
our flesh raw and numb
who provided the match
for her to become a reliable source of warmth
her **burn**
burn
burn

-a mother sets herself on fire//
sacrifice

if you were half as consumed
by the blaze of passion
a quarter as absorbed by your craft
you wouldn't have the attention
nor the regard
to throw shade on what lights us up.

here's to the spark finding you.
-let me be great
(2014)

//excerpt II from *things that will only make sense to him & I* (2010) //

"let go"
"stand back"
"loosen the loving grip"
"our lovers fight their demons
on their own time"
"healing is an inside process"
"you will never be the one who decides
when my peace comes
what it will look like
what it's source will be
or if you will play any role in it's presence"

these are the sentiments his soul screamed-

such a shame-
my teenage heart had gone deaf
-not your wonderwall

am i cruel for failing
to grieve the loss of you..
been too captivated celebrating
the value of me too
-*priorities*

today marked the one hundred and fourth time
that i caressed my own skin

pretending my hands were anyone's
other than his /

the curve of my breast
the supple roundness of my belly
the warm moisture between my thighs /

lifetimes have passed
their touch still feels foreign /

you would think i remain devoted
to a past who never was.
-waiting game

patronizing
demeaning
mocking
the heartwork of another
is no healthy critique

no reflection of your natural subjectivity
your false sense of superiority

are you deaf to the volumes this speaks about you
as a curator.
a pioneer.
an artist.
a human.
-what suzy says of sally (2014)

keep it sexy
but not too sexy

wait
now is not the time to be sexy

stop
these people are not into sexy

chill
now you're too sexy

welp
now you have lost your sexy

oh
that's not sexy anymore

today
well today is a different sexy

what do you mean you don't care about sexy?

-female process of validation

of all the habits i've had the pleasure of unlearning

the pretending won't be missed

i've been overcome by natural responses
been worshipped by a bona fide gentleman
i'll be damned if these curves
don't know the difference
between a boy and a man

i am connected
at last
today my body rejected fraudulent energy
before my spirit even had the chance

you'll never make the cut.
-pathetic penetration

there is a conundrum the philosophers forgot to dissect /

a galaxy of a goddess
faithfully holding hands
with a premature infant of a man

-imbalance//
how they'll remember us (2017)

dad,

you were right.

about prayer.
about fishing.
navigating the sea.
words for therapy.
preserving innocence.
fair-weather friends.
ill-intentioned men.

but not about us.
never about us.
-cult youth

mother nature

mama earth

thank you for this human birth

i am just your student child

let my s u f f e r i n g be mild

-ayahuasca ceremony chant

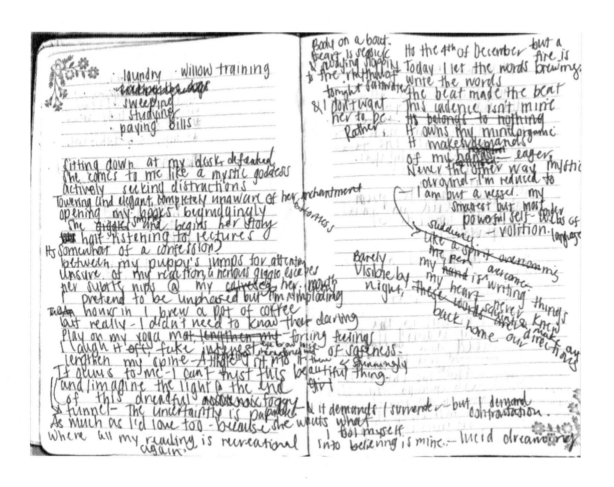

sitting at my wooden desk
defeated.
she comes to me
like a mystic goddess
towering and elegant
this angel is completely unaware
of her enchantment
open my books begrudgingly
she smirks and begins her narrative
half-listening to lectures
is this somewhat of a confession?
between my pups jumps for attention
unsure of my reaction
a nervous giggle escapes her mouth

this tension has a pulse
her subtle nips at my ego
i pretend to be unphased
inside
i am silently imploding
two hours in
i brew a pot of coffee
but really,
i didn't need to know that, darling

play on my yoga mat
forcing feelings of safeness
i laugh it off
fake interest
eyebrow raise here. nod there.
lengthen my spine. a traveling tingle.
i sit into the sensation.
actively seeking distraction
the uncertainty is palpable
imagine the light
at the end of this foggy tunnel
it demands i surrender
i demand confrontation

it occurs to me
i can't trust this stunning creature
as much as i'd love too
because she wants
what i fool myself
into believing is mine.
-lucid dreaming//mistress

they will steal you

at a time when you are untainted

pure love

and they are

insatiable

toxic appetites -

seizing your body /

ravenous,

septic blood -

spreading like cancer /

infectiously invading,

rapidly circulating /

consuming your innocence /

greedy,

starving hearts -

inhabiting your chest cavity /

pounding

with unbearable force /

leaving bruises on your rib cage /

cracking open her defenseless chamber

from the inside out /

and you will scream,

fervently..

"SHAME ON YOU!"

yet –

she will mend.
restore.
develop immunity.
then graciously thank them
for their disease
-plague survival

my sweetest spot

have i foolishly taken you for granted

lost you somewhere along the route

between bleeding

and blooming

rotting

and renewing

between

treachery that hardened me

lessons that seasoned me

cities that loved me

to my very core

seas that soothed my soul

and softened me once more

i've searched through their hearts

buildings

waters

sifted through our past

did this soft fire in my belly

burn you to ash?

-message to [misplaced] inner peace

remember that one time

in my younger days

that i wanted my partner to believe

i loved them so fully

just not quite enough to be genuine?

i betrayed everything i claimed to stand for /

faked deep adoration/

manipulated my intentions /

kicked my lover while they were down /

lied through my teeth /

chuckled at their agony /

fabricated intricate plots

whole universes away from reality/

i scampered away

spinelessly

from any situation that required me to confront my demons /

became violently angry when my deceit was revealed /

i casually put their physical and emotional well-being at risk

via opportunistic filth /

ignored their passions

muted their sentiments

dimmed their light

on the days they didn't have any fight left /

made every hollow attempt to damper their inner fire

that was too rampant for my small mind to wrap around

with the subconscious justification

that it threatened to leave burn marks on my fragile ego /

out loud

i would stage hysterical tears

pleading for forgiveness

blaming each plainly exposed misdemeanor

on my imperfect human nature /

far too intimidated by the thought of confession

to my blatantly weak character /

remember that one time i pretended through it all

because i was too afraid to be authentic

in divulging the uglier parts of me?

me either.

-nothing in common with a coward

before i unlearned
the art of loving quietly
i owned me.
completely.
lotta control.
pinch of passion.
lotta craft.
dash of romance.
simmering independence.

in all that i lacked
i set myself free.
given the chance
i may take her back--
the old me.
-recipe for nostalgia (2016)

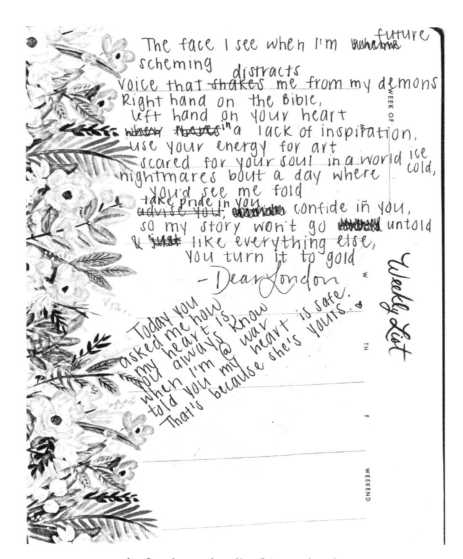

the face i see when i'm future scheming
voice that distracts me from my demons
right hand on the bible, left hand on your heart
in a lack of inspiration, turn your energy to art
scared for your soul in a world ice cold
nightmares bout a day where you'd see me fold
take pride in you, confide in you, so my story won't go untold
and like everything else, you turn it to gold

..today you asked me how my heart is, you always know when i'm at war
told you my heart is safe, that's because she's yours
-dear London
[spoken word & freestyle stand-up recording;
san diego, CA, 2018]

he compliments your beauty
nurtures you like an exotic flower

when the doors shut
does the volume of his voice
bring you to wilt
do his words stab like thorns

he labels you his queen
flaunts you like royalty
when you turn your head
is the throne upheld
do you feel the crown shift
when he betrays you like a peasant…

[be weary of he who is quick
to verbally acknowledge your worth
yet slow to redeem it in moments of truth]
-*imposter*

i collapsed on the shore
defeated

i confessed to mother ocean
each mistake
sin
wrongdoing
blocked blessing
past disgrace

i purged a shameful word vomit of all of my heartache
expecting her to be enraged
and shun me for poor judgment

instead

she mustered all her strength
to split herself wide open
and invite me onto a fresh new land
-healing element//
west coast bound (2017)

A tribute to my father [2002]
The night is long, but the sea is calm
as I stand here at the helm…
And the steady breeze puts me at ease
in a seaman's realm.

The rigging speaks soft moans and creaks,
a product of wind and swell.
Some birds I hear as they fly near
and it's land that their cry do tell.

Yes, it all seems right on this starlit night
all togged up, safe and warm.
But the experienced mind knows that in due time,
there will be another storm.

For come those winter gails that rip your sails
and make the rigging howl,
and waves that heave so high to the darkened sky
that it cramps you in the bowel.

And at sea common trouble can multiply double
And always just when it's least expected…
and though you prepped well for fare or for hell
your best laid plan is rejected.

Three feet of green water on your deck, that's a sight!
Imagine the fear of capsize!
And if she rolls over, will she right?
You'll hold your breath if you're wise.

And you will hold no course to a hurricane's force,
though white-knuckled at the wheel...
Your bare sticks high, and you're wondering why
you ever signed up for this ordeal.

Then she slams with a shudder, now you're light in the rudder
'cause your stern is up in the air!
Next you're on your part side for a downhill slide,
now that's a mix of raw nerve and despair.

Or there's engine room smoke and your steerage is broke
and feel you'll be chucking it in...
or a wintery breeze makes for shivering knees
and ice on your whiskey chin.

Now what? It's a roller coaster ride that wears holes in your hide
and your wet feet are as sore as a boil.
And you're getting no sleep so you're starting to weep
and every small task is a toil.

Now you've popped a main stay
that's swinging wildly overhead
so you're screaming at your deck mate
cause if it hits him he'll be dead…
well he can see you're yelling
with your face all red and scowling,
but the poor fool cannot hear you
with the wind violently howling.

Yes, life is like the sea, my daughter..
sometimes it's calm and serene…
next it's full of strife at the edge of your life
and it all seems a devilish scheme.

You will deal with the worst
perhaps your sight will go first
and your gorgeous blonde hair will start to go gray.
Then overnight, your whole head is white,
and suddenly it's all falling away.

Yet shun remorse and steady your course
the heavens are on your side.
Your days will come when you see the sun
at the changing of the tide.

Fix eyes on the horizon, there's a day star arising
where troubles are all left behind..
then barrel roll towards the sun, your battle is won
and let peace control your mind.

-Life is like the sea," by Weston Mac

i poured my heart & soul onto pen & paper
confronted healthy vulnerability
via blue ink & red wine inspiration

asked God to show me my dirt

watched him rinse it off with soothing dominance
& proceed to challenge me with my treasures

left my soul on my trusted yoga mat
dismissed any pollution of my spirit with every exhale

every detoxifying droplet of sweat
every last tear
of *trauma.*
defeat.
rebirth.
until i couldn't tell the source of the splatter.

'a cleanse,' i told myself,
& i sweated & i cried some more.

forgave myself for any time
i foolishly forgot my worth.
gently brought myself back to center.

made a promise to myself
to keep loni where the light is.

got so drunk i couldn't stand myself.
cried so hard i couldn't recognize myself.
numbed out.
felt again.
relinquished my power.
took it all back.

[kissed the wrong mouth
a combined taste of unspoken guilt

stale perspiration
shitty cologne
i spit him out violently
then hastily came back for seconds]

spoke to my deceased grandmother in a God's dream
felt her humid breath on my ear
her literal & figurative death grip on my wrist
"it's happening...you're happening."

witnessed my sister's seed take some of his very first steps.
spoke words i never imagined admitting out loud
like giving up my most prized possessions.
met with soft relief
as the weight of their attachment made it's exit.

breathed deeply there,
with more peace than it made sense to be experiencing.
a lone wolf,
an alien to my own voyage.
watching, waiting;
full inhale,
& release.

stood defiantly on the forefront of a dream still dreaming.
felt the ever so subtle shift from storm to transition make its entrance.
a complete divine energy transfer, if you will.

waited with a forced sense of patience
on that feeling of cold feet to manifest,
as they all said it inevitably would.

Leapt.
-florida's two week notice (2017)

CIRRUS

chapter 3

Thin, wispy clouds that are high in the atmosphere; so high that they are formed of ice crystals // Indicators of clear, pleasant weather.

on the other side
of excruciating pain

you will find

the sweetest sort of clarity

-watching my sister give birth to a child//

watching my Self give birth to a book

my sun emerged
from the rain clouds today
coaxing me to subdue
she peeked her dazzling light through
to whisper tender affirmations
of a fundamental lost truth
that my Ego had neglected
yet my soul always knew
- *"you'll be okay"*

i frolicked often.
existing in a weightless daze.
s*tep*.
mostly unaware of the living
breathing moment
cocooning my physical existence.
t*wirl*.
only vaguely keen
to my spiritual mission.
to be free. to be me.
if that pronoun may exist
by definition
when the rest falls away.
d*ip*.
to give more
yet take all.
t*ap*.
to disconnect
only to emote more deeply.
s*way*.
to write it down-
because it is forever fleeting.
and i'm not actually paying attention,
anyhow-
just neutrally matching it's frequency.
s*himmy*
this i know for sure
and still-
i know nothing.
p*op*.
sprinkling it with the fairy dust of ignorant
yet decently pure intentions.
shake.
is this getting high?
or getting by?
bow.
-youth as a dance

all that bitter dirt
they fed me...
still I purge sweet
flowers

- lady magic

-lady magic

you, again.

you don't get nearly enough credit.
i've put you through a thousand successions of heaven
and a thousand more of hell.

i still pick you apart,
just because.

and here you are.
resilient as a coffee stain on my favorite damn sweater.

you still look a lot like love.

you sacrifice
you struggle
you evolve.

[i don't deserve you, really.]

-an ode to my mind. body. & heart//
grateful

when i need a backbone of steel
i pray
so the universe channels
the fierce strength of my mother

when i need a heart like the sea
i pray
so the Lord relays
the natural warm tenderness of my father

on the most trying days
when i need to balance both…
-still praying

how do you have

such capacity for hate?

i connect in love languages

i'm struggling to relate.

-language barrier (2015)

you are -
a beacon in the forest
when my sense of navigation has failed me

a refuge
whose door swings open
just as my spirit grows weary and seeks shelter

a swift slap on the wrist
when my capricorn gets the best of me

the heroine of my novel
whom i refuse to disappoint
when giving up grows tempting

my flesh
when i'm desensitized
my oxygenated blood
rushing to my head
when i have run out of breath
my muscles
when i am fatigued

my DNA
when my genetic makeup is compromised
by the demands of society
the stillness behind my zen
the fist behind my fight

i am -
an asylum
when you are a refugee in the country of your own heart

a lighthouse
when the ocean is too vast
for your human vision to grasp

a familiar laugh in a somber moment
a trusted inner compass

reminder of your worth
memoir of your youth

i am a stimulation of your inner child
that innocence you never quite lost

that seldom glare of disapproval
and you know exactly why.
we all say things we don't mean at times.

i am you.

you are me.

and yet.
we are each our own breed of maverick.

an idiosyncratic miracle.

-sister

i once turned an illiterate
raging alcoholic
into an avid poetry reading yogi

then we fell out of love
and went on our merry way
-*writer's fairy tale*

sonríen
brillan
cuentan historias
como si tuvieran sus propias bocas

su magia tan especial.

-los ojos de mi madre

---

rough translation;

they smile
they sparkle
they tell tales
all as if they have their own mouths

what a special kind of magic.

-my mother's eyes

If my story too much for the sane
I rather the psycho in me tell it
let me flirt w/ the pain
off the psychadelics
we are the wordsmiths.

These days I have this nasty habit
where I casually healthy
& walk by good love...
as if its the right size shoe & the price is right
just not for tonight's outfit
occasion

I still have unsung melodies in
my hair
just waiting to find their voice

a warm
cozy
element
like my grandma's humble kitchen

i have just barely inhaled
the scent of your skin
yet i can sense
i have savored it for centuries

each time i stroll into your vibration
the divine goddess in me
is right at home
-*past life reunion* (2017)

2000
you were.
a familiar
genuine
pair of dimples.
an open set of embracing arms
in a sea of strangers.

2005
a dinner table of solace.
a warm homemade meal.
a pillow to rest my head
when my house was not a home.

2009
a protesting advocate
when my solo voice was drowned out.

2011
a sounding board
when the volume of my inner dialogue
became intolerable.

2014
a nomadic companion.
hiking.
picnicking.
giggling
our way across exotic lands.
bold as lions.

year after year -
a dedicated cheerleader
when this world dared to doubt my daydreams…

how many seasons
were you a fortress of unwavering allegiance
when my misplaced sense of loyalty crumbled

how many episodes
when your ego could have reprimanded me with
"i told you…"
rather
your soul affirmed
"i got you."

today
you are a sibling.
you,
who has never shared my blood.

on any given days.
weeks.
months.
that we didn't cross paths
we blossomed in parallel universes -
separate,
but never absent.
never remote.
never
ever
out of reach.

..until our journeys would inevitably intersect once again.

-true friend timeline//
shrivatsa

some of my fondest memories
are inadvertently

my best kept secrets

-shhhh

as a preteen
i was hopelessly conditioned to detest my body
for awkwardly towering over the rest /

fast forward 15 years
it's my very favorite excuse
for living in the clouds
-*woman of stature //*
en las nubes

i tossed my rage to the pacific

i don't need you anymore

you've become my greatest chore

then mother ocean made her vow

not to wash it back on my shore

-liberated

all the cosmos are blushing
when our bodies do
their favorite sunrise dance /
waking up in a sea of pleasure
spine arching
eyes rolling back
before they peeled open
or even had the chance /
who knew.
exiting reality.
is letting you.
enter me.
-daily morning doses (2018)

i expand boldly
shrink discretely
embrace each phase
emit light during darkness
i am most divine by the sea

my forces
determine ocean tides
i eclipse
according to my celestial guides

seen by all
touched by few

i wax
i wane
i am seldom contained

whether i am the faintest sliver
or wildly aglow
the cosmos calculated my phases
i surrender to my perfect flow

let the sun take the day
for a moment in time
only to return within orbit
and resume my night shine
-*moon child*

a mesmerizing catastrophe
exploding with luminosity
radiating as intensely as a billion galaxies
right before abruptly fading to black

angel-
don't weep
we died the way a star might

-supernovae (2014)

waited for a feeling of cold feet that
never quite manifested
I never knew I carried; conquered
others that no longer serve me;
reflected on every intention
I've manifested in the past
3 years that brought me
to this place where I experience
the worst case of cold feet
I've never known, leaped
anyways. got so drunk I
couldn't stand myself;
cried so hard I couldn't (in the
recognize myself. spoke to
my deceased grandmother
in a dream & knew
she told me "this is it."
felt her breath on her ear &
my grip on my wrist - its happening
strong - witnessed my
nephew take some of his
* first steps. most ppl don't
share these things w/ the
world but when you have a
message on your heart,
its just different.
Thanked my body for all it
does for me, all I put it

it's too intimate
it's too troubled
it's too beautiful
it's too innocent
it's too personal
it's too scandalous
it's too painful
it's too private
it's too vulnerable
it's too risky

it's too powerful
yet too defenseless
it's too heavy
it's too disturbing
it's too overwhelming

it's too brainy
but too sexual
it's too bitter
yet it's too sweet

it's too raw
it's too real

it's too **me.**
-project 1 (2018)

imagine
had my grandfather not devised
a plan of timely escape
for my mother and her brothers
with pockets full of mere faith

imagine
had he not secured the safe
peaceful journey
to the foreign land
where she and her daughters
would one day have rights

imagine
had they not committed
to leaving behind relatives
abandoning ancestors
adopting a new tongue
eating new foods
navigating new streets
immersing in what they would consider
a dreadful lack of culture

would i be here
would she be there

the first generation
to never know the third world;
considered a grand blessing

yet here i am
a foreigner on this island
feening for my fix of their hardship

-viva cuba

may you never feel compelled

to pour out

your full

charming heart

to fill a feeble

foul ego

-dear daughter (2014)

your flesh is an oasis
hydrate my physique.
-foreign refreshment

unapologetically *outgrowing*
that which is no longer contributing
to your ascension

saying no
to them
so you may start
saying yes to yourself

distancing
in the areas where you require extra space to grow

no longer recycling
tainted energy
stale thought patterns
that same demoralizing self-talk

forgiving yourself
for those times you so foolishly settled
and those other times
you operated from a place
that felt nothing like love

those times you were flawed
insecure
lazy
downright unkind
the times you were human
(and those other times too)

silencing
when your mind is asking for quiet

listening
when your spirit is demanding attention

sweating
when your body is craving movement

creating
when your soul is aching for expression

watering
the orchids of your life year round
so that your soul's garden may bloom
in every season
-lessons from my mother//
self-love is an inside process

maybe my past ain't a friend
i can call on the phone
if i could i would tell her
darling
take a seat on your throne
check that backbone
it's a quarter past outgrowth
and it's time to come home
-headway and hindsight

i will always sunbathe nude in your light
as shamelessly as you will let me
-*golden lover*

we talk a lot about what makes us tick
i share my childhood self

how pressing my pen to paper
speaking things into existence
without saying a word
was the first and only practice
to elicit that foreign yet intoxicating sensation
that i would later identify as passion

..your brow furrows.
"and what about love?"-
as if to draw a difference

my sweet baby
understand
for me
the two are synonymous
-a wordsmiths's reality (2018)

why guard my heart so desperately
if it's the worthiest asset i have to render
why conceal my soul so protectively
if it is everything i have to be proud of
-*vulnerable by choice*

i rallied all my flaws today
organized them
ranked them by level of severity
and accumulated moments of disservice.

first.
my habit of running.
far.
far.
far as the east is from the west.

worse yet
my habit of staying.
close.
much too close.

followed by my tendency to daydream
my reluctance towards trust
how my heart often spites my hands
for leaving her abandoned
in the custody of the careless and undeserving

this time.
that time.
every time.
every time?

last
my mother's sharp, unpredictable mouth
it's trend towards turning acerbic
how it's gets me into
trouble.
trouble.
unnecessary trouble.
the sort that i secretly live for.

prepped them for battle
sent them off with a sugared smirk
to be suffocated by the nuclear rivals
of enlightened musings
and stubborn aspirations
dripping in golden intentions

-my angels always triumph

you will fight the good fight
in the absence of light
with a certainty
that you are destined to relish rainbows
-walking by faith

i only fell madly in love with my story
once i handed my heart to the narrator

-TO GOD BE THE GLORY

THE ROAR

/ascension/

chapter 4

vibrate higher, moon child.

higher, still.

you owe yourself this frequency.

-glow up

today i became a butterfly

you shamed me for my metamorphosis

why.

if tomorrow you will still be a caterpillar

and i will not shame you for your stagnation

-evolution

forget whatever i said
when i was drunk off ink
and please believe i meant it.

-uncensor my craft

I ate the moon for breakfast
@ 4am before the sun rose
right after I cursed her, under my breath
for glowing joyfully anyway on those who
stole my light —
Now she seeps out of my skin pores
RADIATES through me perpetually
as she selflessly allows me
to shine on them instead

i ate the moon for breakfast at 4am

right after cursing her under my breath

for glowing loyally

on those who stole my light

now

she seeps out of my pores perpetually

selflessly allowing me

to beam on them instead

-chosen one

each time my skin
fuses with his
and our bodies merge
into a single sphere

i catch a rising whisper
resonating through my pores

the sound of my ripe womb
begging us
to make a mother out of her
-maternal clock

you're infatuated with the mere idea of me

how i captain my boat
navigate the seas of my life
establish my own route
make my voyage priority
put the safety of my passengers first

the irony
should i invite you aboard
nominate you co-captain
train you on the languages of my waters
consider your survival paramount

you wouldn't know
the first thing to do in my empire.

it would be
but a matter of time
before you inevitably jumped ship.

-he who wants what he can't have

i used to crave a lover
who would douse my heart in gasoline
light a match
toss it in
burn my embers into his skin
covet the precious scars
never let my dancing flames dwindle

then there was you.

you
who doesn't use profanity -
[only for football]
hair like silk /
beard thick as thieves
sailed the seven seas /
bond over books
read to me while i cook /
crazy good to your mother
could not care less 'bout a past lover /
chuckle when i get crazy
my shit doesn't phase you /

call me at noon to recite my pieces aloud
like making love to my psyche when i'm not around /

earth scented skin
aura so organic /
beer choices are boring
but your foreplay sure isn't /

brew my tea each night
pretend to like hot yoga saturday
never let me miss a worship sunday
joke that these things are my sanity -
we both know that's actually you /

let my inner free bird fly
never questioning her route
nor her anticipated return /

as it turns out
fire was a risky world away from my needs /
who knew you would make a safe
placid
zen
river
out of me /

you bring your guitar to that
one tree
stare in my depths
turn all my stanzas into songs /

humming sweet ripples into my waters
my riverside sweetheart
serenading my reflection
with a combination of our arts /

it's no wonder you're a musician -
hearts weren't made for fires
hearts were made for beats /
-healthy

daddy draws portraits of your smile
and writes poems about your heart.
don't walk to no man down that aisle
unless he makes you feel like art

..though one day your physical beauty
will bring you much attention,
uphold your inner sacred duty-
your spiritual ascension.

and if there comes a day
when you begin to feel unsure,
you are forever the most beautiful
'cause your heart is the most pure.
-daddy's freestyle
(excerpt) (2006)

black power.
white power.
latin power.
*h*umanity *p*ower.

consider me a multicultural cocktail
when you're feening for your fix

and the moment you've neglected the fact
that we all get drunk off the same sloppy love

make that a double.
-polyethnic power

once i accepted i cannot erase foul memories

i mastered shedding their stale energies

-consciousness

enter the jungle
seek a pride of lions
make brothers with the leader
honor the spirit

so that you may master
first-hand
the art of releasing the Ego
when you are loved by a wild thing
-before i'm yours

s c a r e d.

-not i

you have rode shotgun through every tribulation

even when i selfishly neglected to invite you on the journey

for every time my flawed vision failed me without warning

you were there

prepared to casually take the wheel

without ever being asked

you crafted my mind body and soul

with skilled expertise

and guided me in the times i failed to appreciate their perfection

i hastily ignored your advice
on more instances than i would like to admit

you waited patiently

with open arms

for me to come back around

you have never abandoned me

you have never forsaken me

i am as sure as the sunrise

that you never will

i am indebted to you

in this precious, unpredictable life you granted me

and all of the lives to come.

-i serve a faithful God//

Hebrews 13:5

we woke and decided
we were both bigger
and more exquisite
than the small fears
we were set up to inherit
-transgenerational trauma

i once made a promise
that i intend to keep.

a vow that refuses to allow a
racist.

sexist.

homophobic.

misogynist.

bigot.
dull my shine
in the sea of diamonds
that i call my turf
-not my president

i am a fertile ground
for cultivating
seeds of passion's magic /

for the harvests of lush love
i am rich land
yielding a feast /

you will not pollute my soil
with weeds of
half-hearted malnourishment
-love pest

you may not love it

align with it

care for it

you may not fully comprehend it

the sweet and sour vulnerability

the unapologetic calling

but when i peel the layers back to reveal

the uncomfortable

that makes you squirm

the raw

that makes you ill

the ugly

that makes you cringe

only to shake you up

and finish you off

with a flick of the wand that resurrects

a metaphorical wink

and i'm on my way…

-the artist's strategy (2015)

picture a giant bonfire
a quiet confidant in the night
a judgment-free sanctuary
for your tall tales and enigmas

step back in mesmerization of her dazzling
dancing
unpredictability
or simply exploit Her for the warmth
she so eagerly provides

share your musings
inhale the smoke of approval
pay attention to the crackles

[this is how she thanks you
for flammable goods]

just don't get too close
or feed her too much trash
she is known to clap back on invaders

-the fire that is my mind

and if this wild animal that birthed me

be the same epidemic that is my downfall

tell each of my lovers

i dove head first

into my pit of nectar

be sure to

let my momma know

it was a sweet

voluntary demise

-poet's plague

i remember

grappling with my demons

begging them to let me sleep

gasping for air

drowned by my own truth

i remember the day i reclaimed my power.

today

i cruise

windows down

through the mountains and valleys of my psyche

let the pacific kiss my subconscious daily

invite the waves to wash new life into me

when my demons come knocking

i invite them right on in

cork a bottle of malbec

i have shifted this spirit out of shadows

with the guidance of higher frequencies

i have wrote my way into the light

fingertips raw and callused

with my creator as my muse

lifetimes of verses later

you've come to share

a fraction of my sweet solitude

your own slice of my bliss

my question is

in my moments of precious retreat

who are you to feast on a piece

of this peace i earned?

-selfish (2018)

"you are a writer."
"..a speech therapist."
"...a bad bitch!"
"..an aspiring model?"
"...a eurolatina mix?"

i am an ocean at high tide.
i am the faintest sliver of the moon at eclipse.

i am anything but confined -
to my career.
to my hobbies.
to my appearance.
to my ethnicity.

i am a multifaceted multitude of colors.
every museum you said you would one day visit.

i am so,
so many things.

"mommy, what does Loni mean?"
"it means sky in hawaiian, honey. and lion in latin. "

i am the pinnacle of the beast's roar.
i am a gentle drizzle of the rain cloud.

a kaleidoscopic hallucination.
a psychedelic trip.
i am the faintest form of nostalgia
from a whiff of that one fragrance.

i am the melody you sway too.
the beat you nod your head too.

i'm a word smith in a playground
of divine language.
a pioneer on a mission;
*r*escue the *r*eal.

i am none of what you think.

i am the alpha and the omega.
a transcendental representation.
a breathing,
pulsing paradox.
i am a phenomenon in motion.
a wish still wishing.
an orgasm still orgasming.

from the inside out
*f*eel *me* throb.

-s k y l i o n

sky lion

THE AUTHOR

language lover
ocean dweller
third eye advocate
fur momma
great outdoors fan
mental health enthusiast
body activist
travel junkie
self-proclaimed foodie
lover-protector-uplifter
thrill seeker
flower child
feminist

broward county, FL native
san diego, CA resident
florida state university alumni

light distributor.

a million times,
thank you.

sky lion

Made in the USA
Columbia, SC
09 January 2019